New Vanguard • 22

Panther Variants 1942–45

Hilary Doyle & Tom Jentz • Illustrated by Mike Badrocke

First published in Great Britain in 1997 by Osprey Publishing,
Elms Court, Chapel Way, Botley, Oxford OX2 9LP, United Kingdom.
Email: info@ospreypublishing.com

CIP Data for this publication is available from the British Library

ISBN 1 85532 476 8

Series Editor: MARTIN WINDROW

Military Editor: Iain MacGregor
Design: The Black Spot

Filmset in Great Britain
Printed in China through World Print Ltd.

FOR A CATALOGUE OF ALL BOOKS PUBLISHED BY
OSPREY MILITARY AND AVIATION PLEASE CONTACT:

The Marketing Manager, Osprey Direct UK,
PO Box 140, Wellingborough, Northants,
NN8 2FA, United Kingdom.
Email: info@ospreydirect.co.uk

The Marketing Manager, Osprey Direct USA,
c/o MBI Publishing, PO Box 1,
729 Prospect Avenue, Osceola, WI 54020, USA.
Email: info@ospreydirectusa.com

www.ospreypublishing.com

Artist's Note

Readers may care to note the original paintings from which the
colour plates in this book were prepared are available for private
sale. All reproduction copyright whatsoever is retained by the
Publishers. All enquiries should be addressed to:

Mike Badrocke, 37 Prospect Road, Southborough, Tunbridge Wells,
Kent, TN4 0EN

The Publishers regret that they can enter into no
correspondence upon this matter.

PANTHER VARIANTS 1942–45

INTRODUCTION

The theme of this book is the history of the numerous attempts to utilise Panther chassis and Panther components for other weapons systems. Abridged descriptions of the development of various models of the Panther as a tank, and also the Jagdpanther have been included to provide a complete reference work of all Panther variants.

After over 25 years of research, the authors have unearthed thousands of original records from design and production firms, the Heeres Waffenamt (army ordnance department), and the office of the Generalinspekteur der Panzertruppen, General Guderian. Allied wartime reports based on original German records, interviews, and studies of captured equipment have been used to fill in gaps in the history where official German records did not survive the war. The archival research is backed by observations made by the authors climbing over, under, around and through the Panthers, Jagdpanthers and Bergepanthers that still exist in the West. Due to the many misinterpretations in published materials, these have not been used as a source of data in assembling this history of the Panther and its variants.

Following reports from the Eastern Front in 1941 that the German Panzers had been outgunned, the now famous Panther tank was quickly

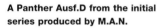

A Panther Ausf.D from the initial series produced by M.A.N.

232296

designed, developed and thrown into production as the new standard medium Panzer. Once the decision was made to proceed with the Panther, the Heeres Waffenamt (army ordnance department), in an attempt to control variations in automotive designs, decided to create a standardised chassis for a range of armoured vehicles based on the new Panther. Those that reached production included Panzerbefehlswagen (command vehicles),

A Panther Ausf.D produced by Henschel in 1943.

Bergepanzer (tank recovery vehicles), Jagdpanzer (tank destroyers) and Panther Ostwallturm (turrets incorporated into fixed emplacements). Proposals for the creation of Panzerbeobachtungswagen (artillery observation vehicles) did not advance beyond a single trials vehicle. None of the many proposals for the Artillerie Selbstfahrlafette (self-propelled artillery chassis) and Flakpanzer (anti-aircraft tanks) utilising automotive components designed for the Panther, entered production.

DEVELOPMENT HISTORY

A special Panzerkommission was summoned to the Eastern Front in November 1941 to visit Guderian's Panzer Armee. A new tank was urgently required to combat the Russian T-34 and KW-1 tanks. The Panzerkommission's report was the basis for Heeres Wa Prüf 6 (the tank design office of the army ordnance department) to contract Daimler-Benz and M.A.N. in December 1941, to design a 30 ton tank mounting a turret with a 7.5 cm Kw.K. L/70. The speed of design was only possible because the Heeres Waffenamt had been working with industrial firms for some time on a series of experimental proposals and developments for various medium tanks.

In March 1942 Speer reported that Hitler had awarded the development contract to Daimler-Benz, but after a technical review the contract went to M.A.N. in May 1942. The decisive factor was the need to get the new tanks into production as quickly as possible, and the Daimler-Benz design required the design of a completely new turret, whereas the M.A.N. Panther could be equipped with an existing Rheinmetall design.

The two prototype V 30.01 (D) with diesel engines which were already being assembled by Daimler-Benz were to be completed for experimental purposes. M.A.N. completed two Versuchs-Panther (experimental Panther chassis) close to the dates ordered, namely August and September. Meanwhile orders had been placed for production of 1,000 Panthers, the first of which was already available in January 1943. This was an amazingly short development period.

Panther Ausf.D

Rheinmetall had designed the turret mounting the 7.5 cm Kw.K.42 L/70, and this was modified for the Panther Ausf.D by eliminating the bulge under the commander's cupola. A 100 mm thick, cylindrical gun mantlet closed off the turret front, which was a 100 mm casting set at an angle of 12 degrees. The turret sides and rear were 45 mm thick at 25 degrees, and the roof 15 mm thick at angles of 84.5 and 90 degrees. Access to the turret was provided through hatches in the cupola and the turret rear. An exhaust fan was mounted on the turret roof.

Adequate vision devices provided the crew in the turret with all-round viewing. The gunner had a binocular TZF12 sighting telescope with 2.5 multi-magnification, and a pistol port to his left. The loader had a pistol port to his right. The commander had all-round vision blocks in the cupola, a pistol port to his rear, and a communication port to his left.

The driver had direct vision through a port cut into the glacis plate, which could be covered with an armoured visor. When the visor was closed the driver used the two fixed periscopes mounted in the super-structure roof. The radio operator could use a port cut in the glacis plate to fire the MG34, and also had two fixed periscopes mounted in the superstructure roof. The maintenance opening in the superstructure roof, initially designed for the removal of the transmission and steering gears, also incorporated hatches for the driver and radio operator.

The driver's front plate was 80 mm thick at 55 degrees, the front nose plate 60 mm at 55 degrees, the superstructure side plates 45 mm at 25 degrees, the hull side plates 40 mm at 0 degrees vertical, the tail plate 40 mm at 30 degrees, the deck plates 15 mm at 90 degrees horizontal, and the belly plate 15 mm horizontal. The superstructure sides were extended out over the tracks to create panniers, limited in their width due to restrictions for rail transport. The width of these side extensions was based on the area needed to house the radiators. The radiators were relocated to positions on both sides so that the centre engine compartment could be sealed leak-tight for deep fording. There was a large, hinged rectangular hatch over the engine compartment. Unlike previous designs where the superstructure was bolted to the hull along a flange, the superstructure was welded to the hull. Access for maintenance of the engine, cooling system, and fuel system was accomplished by unbolting the sections of the rear deck.

The Maybach HL 230 engine was not yet available when production started, so its predecessor the HL 210 was installed. The drive train consisted of the high performance Maybach HL

The rear view of a Panther Ausf.D outfitted as a Panzerbefehlswagen. The Zimmerit anti-magnetic coating was applied at the assembly plants starting in September 1943. The mounting for the Sternantenne D for the Fu 8 radio set is on the rear deck and the 2 m rod antenna on the turret is for the Fu 5 radio set mounted in the turret.

210 P30 12-cylinder motor delivering 650 metric HP at 3,000 rpm through a seven-speed Zahnradfabrik AK 7-200 transmission onto the clutch-brake steering gear and final drives, designed to provide a maximum speed of 55 kilometres per hour. Maintaining the twin torsion bar suspension, the combat weight of 45 metric tons was distributed over eight sets of geschachtelte (interleaved) 860 mm diameter rubber-tyred roadwheels per side. The unlubricated 660 mm-wide tracks provided an acceptable ground pressure (when the tracks sank to 20 cm) of 0.735 kilogram per square centimetre.

Modifications introduced during the production run of the Panther Ausf.D included changing to single-radius steering gear, adding Schürzen protective skirts, reinforcing the roadwheels with 16 rivets between the 16 rim bolts, changing to the 700 metric horsepower Maybach HL 230 engine, dropping the smoke candle dischargers, the communications port, the right headlight, and adding a ring mount on the commander's cupola for an anti-aircraft machine gun.

About 850 Panther Ausf.D were produced by M.A.N., Daimler-Benz, Maschinenfabrik-Niedersachsen-Hannover (MNH) and Henschel in Fgst.Nr. series 210001 to 210254 and 211001 to 214000.

Panzerbefehlswagen Panther (Sd.Kfz.267 und 268)

The command versions of the Panther were produced by modifying the basic design slightly to accommodate additional radio sets. Due to the large space needed to mount the additional radio sets and associated generator, ammunition stowage was reduced to 64 main gun rounds. The coaxial-mounted machine gun was omitted and the hole in the gun mantlet sealed with an armour plug.

The Sd.Kfz.267 was outfitted with an Fu 8 (a 30 watt transmitter with medium wavelength receiver, operating in the frequency band 0.83 to 3 Mhz) and an Fu 5 (a 10 watt transmitter with ultra short wave length receiver, operating in the frequency band 27.2 to 33.4 Mhz). The Sd.Kfz.267 can be identified by an Antennenfuss Nr.1 (antenna base, 104 mm-diameter base) mounted on an insulator protected by a large armoured cylinder fitted on the rear deck. A Sternantenne D (star antenna) for the Fu 8 was fitted to this base. A 2 m Stabantenne (rod antenna) for the Fu 5 was mounted on the right rear corner of the turret roof.

The Sd.Kfz.268 was equipped with an Fu 7 (a 20 watt transmitter and ultra short wavelength receiver, operating in the frequency band 42.1 to 47.8 Mhz) and an Fu 5. The Sd.Kfz.268 can be identified by the 1.4 m Stabantenne for the Fu 7 mounted on the rear deck and a 2 m Stabantenne for the Fu 5 mounted on the turret roof.

Panther Ausf.A

The second production series of the Panther was designated the Ausf.A. A new turret was designed for the Panther Ausf.A, but it retained the same chassis as the Panther Ausf.D. The hull, chassis, drive train and suspension of a Panther Ausf.A produced in September 1943 were exactly the same as the components in a Panther Ausf.D produced during the same month. The main changes introduced with the new turret design were the cast commander's cupola with seven periscopes, a fixed periscope added on the turret roof for the loader, redesigned seals behind the gun mantlet, redesigned seals for the turret race, simplified elevating gear for the gun, and a variable speed turret traverse drive based on the engine speed.

Until November/December 1943, the Panther Ausf.A retained the 'letterbox' flap covering the aperture in the glacis plate through which the radio operator fired the hull machine gun, the TZF12 monocular gun sight, and pistol ports on the turret sides. The main recognition feature for the Panther Ausf.A is the cast commander's cupola, which wasn't present on any of the Panther Ausf.D. However, the key improvement over the Panther Ausf.D was the variable speed turret traverse drive, which theoretically enabled faster target acquisition by the gunner.

Modifications introduced during the production run of the Panther Ausf.A included applying Zimmerit anti-magnetic coating, changing to the monocular TZF12a gunsight, adding a ball mount for the hull machine gun, dropping the pistol ports on the turret sides and rear, adding cooling pipes for the left engine exhaust, welding a tow coupling to the engine access hatch on the hull rear, installing a Nahverteidigungswaffe (close defence weapon) on the right rear of the turret roof, and welding Pilze sockets on the turret roof to be used for mounting the 2-ton jib boom.

About 2,200 Panther Ausf.A were produced by M.A.N., Daimler-Benz, Demag, and Henschel in Fgst.Nr. series 210255 to 211000 and 151000 to 160000.

Panther II

Concerned that the armour protection on the Panther was not sufficient for future conditions on the Eastern Front, Hitler agreed in January 1943 to increase the frontal armour from 80 to 100 mm, and the side armour from 40-45 to 60 mm. This was the official origin of the Panther II. As originally envisioned, the only difference between the designs for the Panther I (Ausf.D) and the Panther II was the armour thickness. All automotive and armament components remained the same. Delivery of the first production series Panther II was originally scheduled for

Close-up of a Panther turret outfitted as a Panzerbefehlswagen. The opening for the co-axial machine gun has been plugged and a mount for the 2 m rod antenna on the turret is for the Fu 5 radio set mounted in the turret.

September 1943. However, if this had actually gone ahead, the Panther Ausf.G and F would never have existed.

Plans had already been made in February 1943 to completely redesign the Panther II and to standardise it with the Tiger II design. As many components as possible were to be shared between the Tiger II and the Panther II. Even the turret design was to be modified. In March 1943, plans for starting production of the Panther II were set back to early 1944. By late April/early May 1943, there was no longer any support for production of the Panther II. M.A.N. was given permission to complete the two Panther II Versuchs-Fahrgestell (experimental chassis) that had been ordered, but no turret design was ever completed or manufactured for the Panther II.

Directly after the war, when questioned by the Allies whether any Panther II had ever been employed in combat, M.A.N. representatives replied: Two experimental Panther II were ordered, although only one experimental chassis was completed. It is possible that this single experimental vehicle could have been employed in combat. The only Panther II Versuchs-Fahrgestell (with a Panther Ausf.G turret that had been completed in March/April 1945 mounted on it) was shipped to Aberdeen Proving Grounds after the war. Large ring wingnuts were present on the Panther II chassis when it was sent to Detroit for testing; the Ausf.G turret was mounted in the USA after 1945. The Panther II Versuchs-Fahrgestell was transferred to the Patton Museum in Fort Knox, where it underwent restoration and is currently on display.

Panther Ausf.G

A new simplified hull design with the superstructure side made from a single plate was introduced on the Panther Ausf.G. The rear deck was also redesigned with a new cooling air intake and armoured exhaust louvres. Also, the driver's and radio operator's hatches were hinged on the outer side, and the driver's visor was replaced by a pivoting traversable periscope. The main drive train and suspension components were kept unchanged from the Panther Ausf.A. The same turret designed for the Panther Ausf.A was retained on the Panther Ausf.G. A Panther Ausf.G produced in April 1944 had the same turret as a Panther Ausf.A produced the same month.

Modifications introduced during the production run of the Panther Ausf.G included changing to welded armour guards to protect the exhaust pipes,

As many chassis components as possible were standardised between the Panther II and Tiger II. The Panther II was designed as a more heavily armoured version. Plans for series production were cancelled after Schürzen side skirts had solved the problem of Russian anti-tank rifles penetrating the 40 mm hull side of the Panther I. Two trial chassis of the Panther II were to be completed for test purposes. After the war one was taken to the USA and is currently on display at the Patton Museum at Fort Knox. The Panther Ausf.G turret was fitted onto this Panther II chassis by the Americans after its capture.

adding sheet metal shields around the exhaust pipes, welding Pilze sockets to the turret roof, fastening a rain guard over the driver's periscope, welding a debris guard over the gap behind the gun mantle, ceasing application of Zimmerit anti-magnetic coating, mounting the FG 1250 infra-red searchlight and scope, changing to Flammvernichter (flame arresting) mufflers, deleting the rear shock absorbers, introducing the 'chin' gun mantlet, mounting a tower over the left engine cooling fan for the Kampfraumheizung (crew compartment heater), and welding five loops for holding camouflage on each turret side.

About 2,950 Panther Ausf.G were produced by M.A.N., Daimler-Benz, and MNH in Fgst.Nr. series 120301 to 130000 from March 1944 and continuing until the assembly plants were captured by the Allies in April 1945.

Panther Ausf.F

Wa Prüf 6 issued a specification for development of a new turret that would overcome a number of problems identified in the existing Panther turret. The most important requests were to eliminate shot deflection underneath the gun mantlet, increase armour protection without increasing overall weight, reduce the frontal area, and internally mount a range finder.

In February 1944 Rheinmetall completed a conceptual drawing of a new turret design which reduced the width of the turret front and gun mantlet, and included an internally-mounted range finder as well as a periscopic gunsight. The range finder was accommodated by creating a massive hump in the turret roof. The Rheinmetall design was not exactly what Wa Prüf 6 had in mind, however, and Daimler-Benz was awarded contracts to complete a new turret design, designated Schmalturm (narrow turret).

The width of the turret was reduced by redesigning the gun mount, and relocating the recoil cylinder and recuperator below the gun instead of on either side. Armour protection for the Schmalturm consisted of a 120 mm-thick front plate at an angle of 20 degrees, 60 mm-thick side and

Starting late in 1944, some Panther Ausf.G were outfitted with the 'FG 1250' infra-red searchlight and scope. The FG 1250 was mounted on a rotating ring inside the upper lip in the commander's cupola. A steel band, threaded through a hole in the turret roof, connected the infra-red sensing scope to a device for sensing changes in the gun's elevation.

rear plates at an angle of 25 degrees, and a 40 mm thick flat roof plate. Armament consisted of the 7.5 cm Kw.K.44/1 L/70 gun with a coaxial mounted MG42. A new stabilised, periscopic SZF1 gunsight was designed with the head protruding through the turret roof. The commander's cupola still had seven periscopes. In comparison to the cast commander's cupola on the Panther Ausf.A and G, the commander's cupola on the Schmalturm was lower, had a hinged hatch, and was drilled so that a TSF1 spotting periscope could be raised without opening the commander's hatch. The fume extraction fan was relocated to the turret base plate to the right of the gun instead of on the turret roof.

The new Panther created by mounting the new Schmalturm on a modified Panther Ausf.G chassis was officially designated the Panther Ausf.F. In addition to the Schmalturm, the following changes were introduced with the Panther Ausf.F: a 25 mm-thick hull roof plate, sliding hatches for the drivers and radio operators, a ball-mounted MP44 in the hull front, easy conversion to a Panzerbefehlswagen by mounting the long range sets in the turret, and all accessories needed to mount the FG1250 infra-red night-sighting equipment.

As planned in October 1944, delivery of the completed Panther Ausf.F was to start at Daimler-Benz in March 1945. However, production was delayed by bombing raids. Panther Ausf.F chassis and turrets were on the assembly line at Daimler-Benz in April 1945. If Daimler-Benz did manage to complete a few Panther Ausf.F between 20 and 23 April 1945, their operation would have been impaired because key components were not available for the Schmalturm, including the range finders and gunsights.

The Panther Ausf.G turret would not fit on the Panther Ausf.F chassis without altering the turret race and turret drive, and this at a time when there were constant power failures. If this had been done at Daimler-Benz, as representatives from M.A.N. stated when interrogated directly after the war, the end result would have been just like any other Panther Ausf.G, but with sliding hatches and an MP44 ball mount. When they were interrogated after the war, Daimler-Benz representatives were not asked about, nor did they comment on, their success in producing a few Panther Ausf.F at the Daimler-Benz assembly plant in Berlin-Marienfelde.

PLANNED MODIFICATIONS

A report on the development emergency programme dated 20 February 1945 consisted of three lists of inventions that were under production. The first list contained those inventions that could have a decisive impact in the near future and were to be given top priority. This list included the month in which the design was to be completed and acceptable for production; the actual date in which it could have entered series production would have been much later. Innovations for the Panther series that were included in the first list were:

1. A Mehrladeeinrichtung (automatic loader) 7.5 cm Kw.K.42/2 (L/70) (to be completed in April 1945)
2. Stabilised gunsights (to be completed in April 1945)
3. Biwa infra-red scope and searchlight and a built-in range finder (to be completed in April 1945)
4. Gummisparende Laufrollen (rubber saving, steel-tyred roadwheels) for all Panzers (to be completed in May 1945)
5. Dreschflegelpanzer (mine-clearing flail tank) (not before May 1945)
6. A 900 metric horsepower Maybach-Motor HL 234 engine (to be completed in August 1945)

The main feature of the Panther Ausf.F was the new Schmalturm (narrow turret). This test vehicle consisted of a Versuchs-Schmalturm mounted on a Panther Ausf.G chassis. Assembly of Panther Ausf.F components commenced at Daimler-Benz just before the end of the war.

The second list consisted of inventions that held promise of special advantages in the future. These projects could not be abandoned without considerable loss of technical and development work and this work was unlikely to be quickly recouped. These were all long-term projects that had no chance of being implemented in the near future. Inventions for the Panther series that were included in the second list were:

1. The air-cooled Simmering diesel engine and the water-cooled Deutz diesel engine
2. Stabilised tank guns
3. Hydrostatic steering units for the Panther
4. Hydrodynamic steering units for the Panther
5. Panther-Turm with 8.8 cm Kw.K. L/71

The third list consisted of inventions for which development work was to cease immediately. There was only one invention on the third list from the Panther series: the s.F.H.18 auf Panther-Bauteilen (15 cm howitzer self-propelled chassis designed with Panther components).

BELOW, LEFT A close-up of a Panther Ausf.F turret which was shipped to the USA for evaluation after the war. This turret has a normal monocular gun sight to the left of the opening for the gun mount. (Tank Museum)

BELOW, RIGHT A close-up of the production turret for the Panther Ausf.F which was shipped to England for evaluation after the war. (Tank Museum)

BERGEPANTHER

On 29 March 1943, the Generalinspekteur der Panzertruppen, General Guderian, ordered that out of the monthly Panther production, four per cent plus three vehicles were to be completed without turrets and so equipped that they could be used in the interim as Panzer-Bergegerät (tank recovery vehicles) in the Panzer-Abteilungen. Since it had designed the basic Panther chassis, M.A.N. was given a contract for the detailed design for the Bergepanther. On 10 May 1943, M.A.N. was ordered to complete ten Bergepanther to be delivered by 6 June 1943. These first Bergepanther were merely normal Panther chassis without their turret and with improvised decking over the turret ring. Twelve of the Panther Ausf.D chassis were completed (with Fgst.Nr. from 120125 to 120137) without turrets or winches and delivered in early June 1943.

By 12 May 1943, Henschel had been notified that they were to complete their second production series of Panthers (Ausf.A) as 70 Bergepanther (Fgst.Nr. 212131 to 212200). The production schedule specified that the first nine were to be delivered in June 1943, followed by 11 in July. On 15 June, Henschel reported that it was impossible to meet the deadline. At their meeting on 28 May 1943 at M.A.N., Henschel had been informed that the design of the chassis including the winch should not be expected until the end of June.

The Bergepanther chassis design was sufficiently altered to receive its own drawing/part number series 021St41860. The armoured hull (drawing/part number 021St41861) was extensively modified for mounting recovery equipment and was welded together as a separate series of hulls by the armour manufacturer Ruhrstahl.

The rough layout created by M.A.N. in drawing number Tu 15411 dated 19 June 1943 shows some of the components specifically designed for the Bergepanther, including:

1. A 2 cm Kw.K. gun with an armour shield (021St41870) mounted on the glacis
2. A winch with 40 ton draw and accessories (021St41875 –41878) mounted in the centre of the hull

A Bergepanther based on the Panther Ausf.A (Fgst.Nr. 175644). This vehicle was captured and brought to England for examination. (Tank Museum)

3. A built-up superstructure called a bridge (021St41874) which was decked with steel-framed planks and had folding wooden sides

4. A lifting derrick with base mounts on both sides (021St41879)

5. A cable guide (021St41880) mounted on the rear deck

6. A large spade (021St41869), hinged to the bottom of the hull rear, served as a ground anchor

7. A tow coupling (021St41872) bolted to the hull rear and belly

8. A tow coupling bolted (021St41873) to the nose on the front.

The front tow coupling did not get into production. It was replaced by two studded plates welded to the nose for anchoring the large wooden beam used for pushing other vehicles. Other component parts specifically designed for the Bergepanther included the engine exhaust (021St41863), fuel tanks (021St41864), crew seats (021St41867), base mounts for an anti-aircraft machine gun (021St41871), a device to measure pulling power (021St41885), a hydraulic pump and drive (021St41886) and an oil cooling system (021St41888). All other components for the suspension, drive train, and rear deck had drawing/part numbers in the 021St48300 series, having been adopted from (and being interchangeable with) the Panther Ausf.D.

The winch was installed in the space originally used for the tank fighting compartment and was enclosed by the box-like superstructure, 32 in high, 8 ft 1 in wide and 7 ft 6 in long. A top was built in over the winch compartment, 16 inches above the top of the hull, and the upper halves of the sides were hinged from it. The open compartment formed by the hinged sides was used for the stowage of accessories and equipment. The winch had a capacity of 40 metric tons on a straight pull, and 80 tons when using a pulley in the line. It was driven through a transfer case in the drive shafts from the engine. The winch control levers were located in the crew compartment. A lever under the right personnel seat operated the dog clutch for engaging the winch drive and two levers on the right controlled the winch clutches and brake. Many of

the second series of the Bergepanther Ausf.A and the Bergepanther Ausf.G were completed and delivered without a winch installed.

The simple derrick rigged with a block and tackle was used for lifting heavy equipment. It could be mounted on either side by means of brackets welded to the superstructure side plates. The equipment and accessory stowage layout and the design of the spade were changed after Demag took over production of the second series of Bergepanther Ausf.A (Fgst.Nr. 175501-175663) from Daimler-Benz in March 1944.

A Bergepanther based on the Panther Ausf.G. This vehicle was used after the war by the French Army. The 2 cm Kw.K gun mount has been dropped.

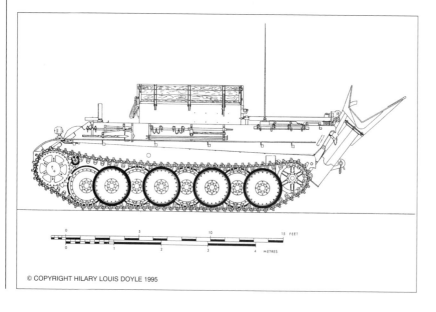

1:76 scale side view drawing of a Bergepanther Ausf.G. (Hilary Louis Doyle)

The Bergepanther Ausf.G (Fgst.Nr. series starting with 175664) was assigned drawing/part numbers in series 021St51430. The only component parts specifically designed for the Bergepanther Ausf.G were the armour hull (021St51431), mounts for components in the hull (021St51432), the brake and transmission fume exhaust system (021St51433), the engine exhaust (021St51434), the fuel tanks (021St51435), the electrical equipment (021St51436), the radio racks (021St51437), the external mounts and clamps (021St51438), and the air filter regulator (021St51439). All of the other components associated with the suspension, drive train, and rear deck were adopted from and were interchangeable with the same components for the Panther Ausf.G. The rest of the equipment and accessories for recovery operations had the same drawing/part number as those that had been designed for the Bergepanther Ausf.A. Even the 2 cm Kw.K. gun mount was included on the drawing list dated 15 October 1943, although they were dropped during the production of the Bergepanther Ausf.A. The armament for the Bergepanther Ausf.G consisted of an MG34 in the same ball mount as a Panther Ausf.G, and a single base mount for an anti-aircraft machine gun welded to the guard over the radio operator's fixed periscope.

As available, two Bergepanther were to be issued to the recovery section in each Panther-Abteilung, Tiger-Abteilung and schwere Panzer-Jäger-Abteilung (heavy tank destroyer battalion). Bergepanther were also issued to special independent repair and recovery units attached to army commands.

To recover a tank, the Bergepanther was backed into position about 10 metres from the disabled tank and the winch was used to lower the spade. Both ends of a tow cable were attached to the tank and the cable placed over a pulley. The eyelet of the winch cable was then attached to the pulley. To play out cable, the winch brake was released, the winch clutch lever placed in neutral and the Bergepanther driven forward in first gear until a suitable piece of ground was reached. The spade would drag on the ground.

To winch a disabled tank, the brakes of the Bergepanther were set and the winch operated. If the brakes were insufficient to hold the

Bergepanther, it slid back until the spade dug in. If the load on the cable exceeded 40 tons, a warning signal lit up and the winch was stopped. By attaching a second pulley to the one on the tow cable, passing the winch cable through it and anchoring the end of the winch cable to the tow coupling on the Bergepanther, the towing power was raised to 80 metric tons. If the warning signal again lit up, a second Bergepanther had to be used. To tow a disabled tank after recovery, two towing bars were attached to the front of the tank and to the tow coupling on the rear of the Bergepanther.

Jagdpanther

Searching for a self-propelled mount for the newly-developed long 8.8 cm gun, the Heeres Waffenamt decided on 3 August 1942 to utilise the Panther chassis. At first the job of designing this Jagdpanzer was awarded to Krupp, which had been working on designs to mount the 8.8 cm gun on a modified Pz.Kpfw.IV chassis. Krupp determined that the Panther chassis would have to be significantly modified and they would be unable to deliver the construction drawings until January 1943. A one-tenth scale model was to be completed by the end of September, and a full-scale model by 10 November 1942. The Waffenamt wanted the first vehicle completed in June 1943, with series production starting in July.

During a meeting at Speer's Reichsministerium für Rüstung und Kriegsproduktion (Reich ministry for equipment and wartime production) on 15 October 1942, it was decided that Daimler-Benz would continue design development of this vehicle, since production was to commence at the Daimler-Benz assembly plant in the summer of 1943. Krupp, assisting Daimler-Benz with the design of the vehicle and maintained primary responsibility for the design of the gun and gun mount. Even though Krupp was relieved of primary design responsibility, they completed their version as a full-scale wooden model and presented it to the Waffenamt on 16 November 1942. This model, with its low silhouette, had very little resemblance to the final design for the Jagdpanther.

At a meeting at Daimler-Benz in Berlin on 5 January 1943, several technical points in the design of the 8.8 cm Sturmgeschütz (the original name for the Jagdpanther) were established. The upper front plate was to be 100 mm thick and the lower front plate 60 mm thick, both laid back at an angle of 55 degrees from the vertical. The top, bottom and rear plates were to be 30 mm thick. The gun mantlet was to be a molybdenum-free steel casting bolted to the front plate so that the gun could be readily dismounted. If the transmission and steering gear could be removed through the aperture for the gun mount, the superstructure roof was to be welded in place. Instead of a visor, two periscopes were to be mounted in the front plate for the driver, and pistol ports would provide vision to the side. The first armoured hulls were to be completed by the armour manufacturer by the middle of 1943 and the first production series vehicle completed in December 1943.

At a conference with Hitler on 6 March 1943, the designers decided to examine the gun mantlet for the Sturmgeschütz auf Panther to see whether it was possible to use the same type of ball-mount design as in the Porsche Sturmgeschütz. They wanted to avoid creating a shot trap on the gun mount, as in the Sturmgeschütz auf Pz.Kpfw.III Fahrgestell.

A Waffenamt specification dated 1 May 1943 for the 8.8 cm Panzerjäger 43/3 L/71 auf Panther Fahrgestell included the following details. The armour thicknesses for the superstructure were 100 mm at 55 degrees for the front, 60 mm at 35 degrees for the side, 40 mm at 35 degrees for the rear, and 30 mm at 80 degrees for the roof. The armour thicknesses for the hull were 60 mm at 55 degrees for the lower front plate, 60 mm at 0 degrees for the sides, 40 mm at 35 degrees for the rear, and 30 mm at 90 degrees for the deck and belly. The vehicle had the same armour thicknesses and shape as the hull for the proposed Panther II. In addition to the 8.8 cm Pak 43/3 main gun, an MG34 and two machine pistols were to be carried inside the vehicle. Vision devices included a periscopic Sfl.Z.F.5 gunsight for the gunner, an SF14Z scissors periscope for the commander, and seven additional periscopes for the crew. A crew of five was specified, consisting of the commander, gunner, driver, and two loaders. The radio sets, Fu 15 and Fu 16, were those commonly used by the artillery, not the Panzertruppen. The battery and Abteilung commander's vehicles were to be outfitted with an additional long range radio set, the Fu 8.

By 4 May 1943, it had been decided to continue production of the Panther I. The Panther II design was to be shelved and it was not to be mass-produced. Since the original design basis used by Daimler-Benz had been the Panther II hull, the firm was now ordered to revise the design and base it on the Panther I chassis, but to incorporate the simplifications introduced into the Panther II design. These changes were to be quickly implemented so that the first hulls could be delivered by the armour manufacturer in September. The new armour thicknesses were 80 mm for the superstructure front, 50 mm for the lower hull front and superstructure sides, 40 mm for the superstructure rear, hull sides, and hull rear. The roof and belly plates were to remain 30 mm thick. The drive train and suspension were the same as in the Panther I.

This first Jagdpanther test vehicle was produced in late 1943. It features a monobloc gun tube for the 8.8 cm Pak 43/3 L/71, double periscopes for the driver, and pistol ports on the superstructure sides.

A rear view of one of the last Jagdpanther. This vehicle has the heating tower over the left fan outlet from the motor. The Flammvernichter (flame suppressor) on the exhaust pipes even have the hoods fitted.

Due to the limited space at the Daimler-Benz Werk 40 assembly plant in Berlin-Marienfelde, and problems that Daimler-Benz encountered in meeting production quotas for the Panther, by 24 May 1943 a decision was made to have the schwere Sturmgeschütz produced at Mülhenbau und Industrie A.G. (Miag) in Braunschweig. The armour thicknesses of the roof, rear deck, and belly plates were reduced to 16 mm in order to cut the overall weight of the vehicle. Because the gun had been offset to the right of the vehicle's centreline to allow additional room for the driver, traverse had been reduced from 14 degrees to 12 degrees to the right and left.

By 9 June 1943, the specification listed a crew of six (with the addition of a radio operator), ammunition stowage for 50 rounds for the main gun, 30 rounds for the Nahverteidigungswaffe, 600 rounds for the loosely carried MG42, and 760 rounds for four MP40. The periscopic Sfl.Z.F.1a was to be mounted as the main gunsight. The head of this periscope extended through an aperture in the superstructure roof and traversed with the main gun. Vision devices were limited to two periscopes for the driver, five pistol ports, an SF14Z(Sfl.) scissors periscope, and two periscopes for the loaders. Three access hatches were provided for the crew: one at centre right in the roof for the commander, one at the left rear in the roof above a loader, and one centred in the superstructure rear.

A full-scale model of the Panzerjäger mit 8.8 cm L/71 auf Panther had been completed by Daimler-Benz in June and was transferred to Miag to aid in completing assembly drawings and procedures. This same model was displayed to Hitler on 20 October 1943 along with wooden models of the Tiger II and Jagdtiger.

The Germans learnt on the Ferdinand at Kursk that a machine gun was needed to engage infantry and other soft targets, so an MG34 was mounted in the superstructure front to the right of the main gun in the same ball mount introduced with the Panther Ausf.A. Other design modifications introduced prior to the production of the first

Two Jagdpanther passing through a town in France in 1944. These Jagdpanther still have the small opening in the front plate for the gun and the monobloc single piece 8.8cm. The second periscope opening has been closed off. (Bundes Archiv)

Versuchs-Jagdpanther were: a reduction in crew numbers from six to five, an increase in the number of main gun rounds carried from 50 to 60, and a reduction in the number of periscopes in the superstructure roof from five to four, of which two were fixed and two were rotatable.

The drive train and suspension were exactly the same as in the Panther. The high-performance Maybach HL 230 P30 12-cylinder motor delivered 700 metric HP at 3,000 rpm through a seven-speed Zahnradfabrik AK 7-200 transmission onto the single-radius steering gear and final drives, designed to provide a maximum speed of 55 kilometres per hour. All transmissions inside the seven surviving Jagdpanther examined by the authors were normal production series AK 7-200 transmissions. As a modification during the production run, the final drives were strengthened because of numerous failures.

The first Versuchs-Jagdpanther was completed at Miag in October and the second in November 1943. A letter dated 29 November 1943, later reprinted by the OKH on 1 February 1944, listed the suggested names for several armoured vehicles, including Jagdpanther, as the official name for the schwere Panzerjäger 8.8 cm auf Panther I.

Modifications during the production run of the Jagdpanther included: dropping the pistol ports, adding a Nahverteidigungswaffe (close defence weapon) mounted on the superstructure roof, deleting the left driver's periscope, adding a towing bracket welded to the engine access hatch on the hull rear, relocating the jack, adopting components on the rear deck from the Panther Ausf.G, adding cooling pipes for the left side engine exhaust manifold, introducing the sectional monobloc 8.8 cm Pak 43/3 gun, ceasing the application of Zimmerit anti-magnetic paste, strengthening the outer gun mantlet, adding sheet metal shields to the engine exhaust pipes, introducing a larger diameter, self-cleaning idler wheel, deleting the rear shock absorbers, introducing Flammvernichter (flame arresting) mufflers, mounting a tower over the left engine cooling fan for the Kampfraumheizung (crew compartment heater), and dropping the stowage bin that had been mounted behind the superstructure.

About 413 Jagdpanther were produced by Miag, MNH and MBA in the Fgst.Nr. series starting with 300001 from January 1944 until the assembly plants were captured by the Allies in April 1945.

Initially, the Jagdpanther were issued to the schwere Heeres Panzer-Jäger-Abteilung 654, the only unit to be equipped with three companies of 14 Jagdpanther and the first unit to take them into combat in the West. A single company in each of four schwere Heeres Panzer-Jäger-Abteilungen was outfitted with Jagdpanther and sent to fight in the West. Finally, in January 1945, one company in each of two schwere Heeres Panzer-Jäger-Abteilungen was issued with Jagdpanther and sent to the Eastern Front. From January 1945, Jagdpanther were used to equip one company in several Panther-Abteilungen. Even with their outstanding armament and armour protection, the Jagdpanther had been introduced too late and were too few in number to be more than a local tactical problem for Allied tankers.

In an attempt to develop interest in mounting their 12.8 cm L/55 gun on a Panther chassis, Krupp produced a series of proposal sketches numbered Hln-A 146 and Hln-B 147 on 24 November 1944. These showed a rear-mounted fighting compartment with the motor moved to the middle of the hull. Obviously, such a radical development could not be taken seriously at the time and the idea was dismissed.

Only one variant of the Jagdpanther had been actively pursued: the rigid mounting of the 8.8 cm L/71. Elimination of the recoil gear of a weapon promised savings in materials, weight and production time. Initial work had been carried out mainly on the 7.5 cm L/48 in Jagdpanzer 38(t), but the designers were unable to transfer the lessons learned to the 8.8 cm L/71 on the Jagdpanther. Krupp were involved in preliminary design and development, and proposed mounting the 8.8 cm L/71 further back in the Jagdpanther fighting compartment. Due to the general war situation nothing came of this idea.

FIXED FORTIFICATIONS

Panther Ostwallturm

Panther turrets were installed in fixed fortifications from late in 1943. Some of these were Panther production series turrets, but most were specifically designed for their intended function as traversable gun turrets. The cupola was replaced with a flat hatch, and the turret roof was strengthened with armour 40 mm thick in order to withstand direct hits from artillery shells up to 15 cm. The armour manufacturer Dortmund Hoerder Hüttenverein had completed the armour components for 112 Panther Ostwallturm by the end of February 1944. A second order was placed with Ruhrstahl for the armour components for 155 Panther Ostwallturm to be completed by August 1944. The turrets were assembled as functional units at Demag-Falkansee; they delivered 98 Panther Ostwallturm by the end of May 1944 and were scheduled to continue production at the rate of 15 per month.

Two different emplacements were actually used, one made out of a welded steel box known as the Pantherturm I (Stahluntersatz), and the second with a reinforced concrete base known as the Pantherturm III

(Betonsockel). The Wa Prüf Fest IV (the fortifications design office of the army ordnance office) issued a drawing dated 30 November 1944 for the Panther-Turm A (Schnelleinbau) which shows how to emplace a Panther Ostwallturm on a timber bunker.

The Pantherturm I (Stahluntersatz) emplacement was made in two parts. The upper section, 960 mm deep, was equivalent to the fighting compartment of a tank and the turret was mounted in the 100 mm thick roof. The ammunition was stored around the turret basket. The sides were 80 mm thick, but there was no floor other than under the ammunition bins. This upper box of the emplacement was manufactured by Krauss-Maffei in München.

The lower emplacement box housed the crew quarters with fold-down bunks, a heating stove and a DKW motor powering an electric generator. A large entrance door was protected by a passage within the housing. A small escape hatch was also provided. The steel sides were 70 mm thick and the floor was 40 mm. The lower box had no roof as it was bolted to the upper box after emplacement. The chimney stack for the stove could be removed when not in use.

On 26 March 1945, a total of 268 Panther turrets were reported as having been installed as follows:

	Total	Atlantic Wall and Westwall	Italy	East	Schools or Experimental
Pantherturm I	**143**	119	18	6	0
Pantherturm III	**125**	63	30	30	2

This Panther Ostwallturm was abandoned before it could be mounted on its crew quarters sub-base. It was to be part of the Gothic line in Italy and was photographed in September 1944. The turret was specially produced for static deployment, with 40 mm roof armour and a hatch with a rotating periscope instead of a cupola. (Imperial War Museum)

An Allied report from the Mediterranean Theatre states:

'Panther turrets were first met in the Hitler Line and were in fact the salient features around which the other defences were built up. They are actual tank turrets, though perhaps of a slightly earlier vintage than those now on tanks. They are mounted on a turret ring fitted on an armoured box built up of welded plate about 2.5 inches thick. The whole of this box is sunk into the ground and earth is banked up close to the turret so that it is just cleared by the gun at depression and yet offers some additional protection to the base of the turret skirt. Traverse is by hand only and no power is supplied. Access to the turret is either by the access hatches of the turret itself or from underneath the armoured box by means of a steel ladder communicating with a deep dug-out. It is obvious that the crews live in the turret and dug-out permanently as electric light is supplied and there are other signs of continuous occupation.

'This system of static defence was backed up by self-propelled equipment and ordinary ground anti-tank guns. In front of each position there was a graveyard of Churchills and some Shermans; perhaps eight tanks to a gun and all within 200 yards of it. This is, at present, the cost of reducing a Panther turret and it would seem to be an excellent investment for Hitler. Obviously these turrets are most formidable unless each one is dealt with by a carefully prepared and co-ordinated attack.

'The turrets are almost invisible until they fire and, when located, there is very little to shoot at and, unless the turret happens to be pointing elsewhere, it will not be penetrated either by the 75 mm or 6-Pounder guns. H.E. fire is obviously useless. In all cases there was enough of the turret left to diagnose the method of destruction, pen-etration of the turret side had been effected.

'One Churchill crew who destroyed one with their

A Panther Ostwallturm destroyed by Canadian forces. These bunkers proved most difficult to destroy. This one was hit in the turret side and was blown up when its ammunition supply exploded. (National Archives of Canada)

6-Pounder say that the turret blew up immediately it was hit. This was presumably due to the ammunition, since a large quantity is stored. Certainly the sample in question appeared to have been reduced to its component parts and the gun barrel can still be seen sticking up in the air like a telegraph pole, some distance from the site. If anti-tank defence is to consist of these turrets in the future it cannot but emphasise the need for a proportion of tanks to carry a really effective armour penetrating weapon, though it is not by any means accepted that attack by tanks is the best or correct method of dealing with them.'

PROPOSALS FOR THE ARTILLERY

Panzerbeobachtungswagen Panther

Rheinmetall was assigned detailed design development of a turret for a Panzerbeobachtungswagen Panther (armoured artillery observation vehicle using a Panther chassis). Several variations were considered, including an altered Panther turret with a 5 cm Kw.K.39/1 gun and a coaxial machine gun in a Topfblende (pot mantlet) mounted in the centre of a flat plate covering the front of the turret. This version was identified as Entwurf 3 (third proposal) for an Artillerie-Panzer-Beobachtungswagen Fahrgestell Panther in drawings H-SkB 79557 dated 10/11 November 1942. The design already incorporated a built-in range finder, the TBF2 observation periscope mounted in the turret roof to the right of the commander's cupola, and a TSR1 spotting periscope mounted in the turret roof by the gunner. The commander's cupola shown in the drawing was an interim design with seven periscopes protected by cylindrical armour rings.

As shown on the earliest drawings dated 5 March 1943, the Waffenamt approved development of a different design with a fake gun. Its only armament was a ball-mounted machine gun. This was an original turret design that was assigned a new drawing/part number series (021St50400) with a few of the components borrowed from other Panther turret designs. It was not a turret manufactured for a Panther Ausf.D and then modified to fit the components needed for an observation vehicle. The main armour housing (drawing/part number 021St50401) for the turret retained the same general shape of the Panther Ausf.D turret, but due to the installation of a dummy barrel providing some element of protection, the turret front was closed off by a flat 100 mm thick plate. Other components specifically designed for this turret included:

1. A hatch in the right front of the turret roof for an observer (021St40402)
2. The turret race (021St50403)
3. A dummy gun (021St50404)
4. The ball mount for an MG34 in the turret front (021St50405)
5. A hatch in the middle of the turret roof and mount (021St50406) for the TBF2 observation periscope
6. The floor of the turret basket (021St50407)
7. The turret drive gear (021St50408)
8. A commander's seat (021St50409) centred in the rear, not under the commander's cupola
9. A seat for a radio operator (021St50410) in the right rear
10. A seat for an observer (021St50411) in the right front
11. A platform for the commander to stand on when looking out the open hatch (021St50412)
12. A platform for the observer to stand on when looking out the open hatch (021St50413)

The components adopted from the Panther Ausf.D turret design included:

1. An azimuth indicator (021St48876)
2. The rear access hatch (021St48952)
3. The communication hatch (021St48953)
4. Pistol port plugs (021St48955)
5. The drive (021St48960) for the 12-hour azimuth indicator in the commander's cupola
6. The fume extraction fan (021St48979) (moved to a new location on the right rear corner of the turret roof)

The components adopted from the Panther Ausf.A turret design included:

1. A cast commander's cupola (021St50256) with seven periscopes
2. The turret traverse drive (021St50263)
3. The turret traverse lock (021St50270)

Smoke candle dischargers (021St51406 and 51407) were mounted on the turret sides, even though they had been dropped from Panther and Tiger production in May 1943. All layout drawings for the Turm Panzerbeobachtungswagen Panther had been completed and reviewed by 16 July 1943. A single Versuchsturm (experimental turret) was completed and mounted on a Panther Ausf.D chassis originally produced between July and September 1943.

The dummy gun and mantlet were constructed of welded sheet metal and bolted to the front of the turret. The MG34 was mounted in a ball mounting in the turret front plate to the right of the dummy gun. It was sighted by means of the standard KZF2 sighting telescope. The machine gun could be traversed 5 degrees left and right, and had a maximum depression of minus 10 degrees and elevation of plus 15 degrees. An MP40 was carried loose in the vehicle along with a signal pistol.

The instruments in the Panzerbeobachtungswagen were designed to measure the initial range as well as switches and corrections based on observation of fall of shot for transmission to the artillery. It was equipped with an EM 1.25 m (1.25 metre base) range finder, a TBF2 observation periscope (with a spare), a TSR1 spotting periscope (with a spare), an SF14Z scissors periscope, and a KZF2 telescopic gun sight (with a spare).

The EM1.25 m range finder manufactured by Zeiss was mounted inside across the front of the turret with vision slots cut into the front plate for the instrument. These slots could be closed by hinged cover plates from within the turret, and there was armour protection behind them in the turret front plate which could be dismantled when the range finder was removed and installed. The graticules on the range finder could be illuminated for use in dim light.

The TBF2 observation periscope was mounted in the centre of the turret in a ball mounting in the roof plate. Counterbalanced by an elaborate rig of pulleys and counterweight, it could be raised and lowered through 37 centimetres, traversed through 360 degrees and tilted through 10 degrees. When it was in the lowered position, the opening in the roof above the periscope could be closed by a hinged cover plate. The TSR1 spotting periscope or the SF14Z scissors periscope was mounted on an adjustable bracket inside at the base of the commander's cupola.

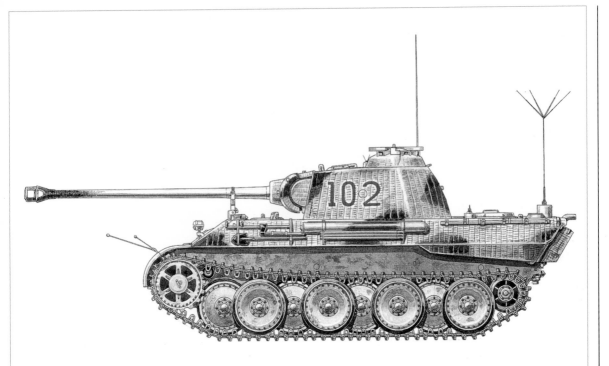

1: Panther Ausf.A as a Panzer-befehlswagen, Panzer-Regiment 4, Anzio, Italy, 1944

2: Panther Ausf.G mit FG 1250, October 1944

A

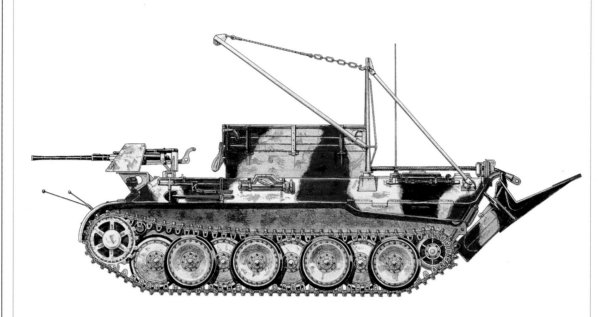

1: Bergepanther, September 1943

2: Panther Ostwallturm, Gothic Line, Italy 1944

Jagdpanther, Ardennes, December 1944

C

PANTHER AUSF.G mit FG 1250
OCTOBER 1944

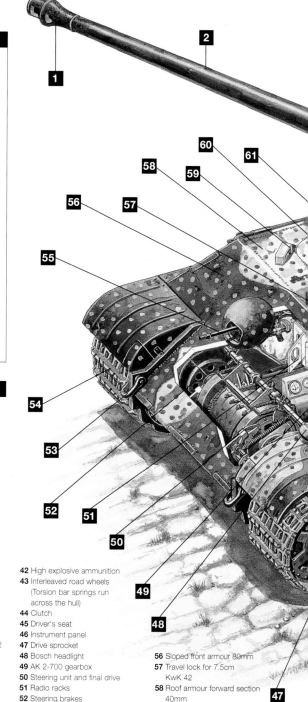

KEY

1 Muzzle-brake
2 7.5cm KwK L/70
3 Sheet metal cover to prevent dirt fouling gun mantlet
4 Gun mantlet
5 T.Z.F 12a gunsight
6 Traverse motor
7 Recoil system for 7.5cm KwK L/70
8 Fume extractor
9 Strap from FG 1250 Infrared sight to the gun
10 Search light with infrared filter
11 FG 1250 Infrared sight
12 Loader periscope
13 FG 1250 mounting attached to rotating ring in commander's cupola
14 Nahverteidigungswaffe (Close in defence rotating grenade launcher)
15 Right hand side engine cooling extractor fan armoured cover
16 Right hand side/ rear cooling air intake grill
17 Fuel tank overflow/ vent
18 2 meter rod antenna for FuG. 5 radio system
19 Storage bin
20 Oil bath air filters over carburettors of Maybach HL 230 P motor

21 Armoured fuel filler cap
22 Radiator water filler cap
23 Exhaust pipes
24 Stowage bin
25 Sloped side pannier armour 50 mm
26 Left hand side/ rear radiator
27 Left hand side engine cooling extractor fan
28 Left side pannier fuel tank
29 Adjustable idler wheel
30 Spare track links
31 Turret escape hatch
32 Cleaning rods and spare antenna rod container
33 Ring on commander's cupola for mounting anti-aircraft machine gun mount
34 GG 400 generator to drive the Infra-red search light
35 Commander's cupola pivoting hatch
36 Recoil guard on 7.5cm KwK 42
37 Turret ring ball bearing race
38 Commander's cupola with 7 periscopes
39 Armour piercing ammunition Pzgr.39/42 in pannier racks
40 Central lubrication unit
41 Schürzen, 5mm armoured apron to protect 40mm side armour from anti-tank rifle fire

42 High explosive ammunition
43 Interleaved road wheels (Torsion bar springs run across the hull)
44 Clutch
45 Driver's seat
46 Instrument panel
47 Drive sprocket
48 Bosch headlight
49 AK 2-700 gearbox
50 Steering unit and final drive
51 Radio racks
52 Steering brakes
53 Tow cable shackles
54 660mm wide track
55 MG 34 machine gun in armoured ball mount

56 Sloped front armour 80mm
57 Travel lock for 7.5cm KwK 42
58 Roof armour forward section 40mm
59 Fixed periscope for radio operator
60 Radio operator's hatch
61 Main roof armour 16mm

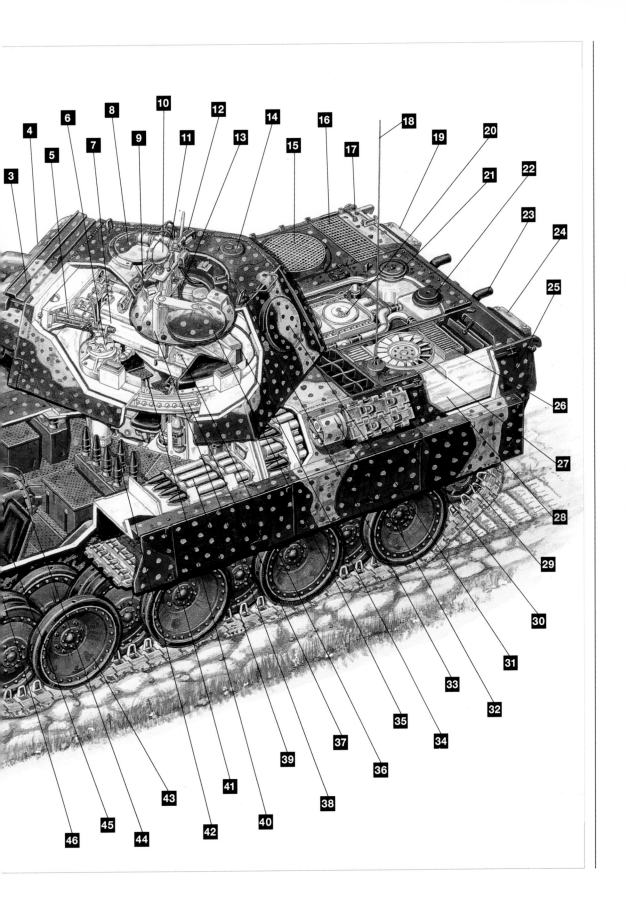

Panzerbeobachtungswagen Panther, 1943

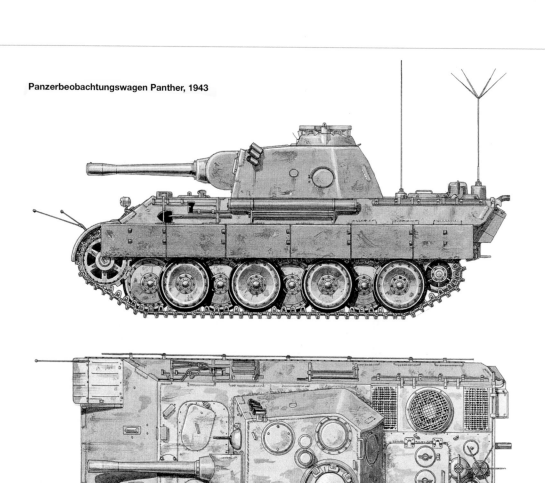

3.7 cm Flakpanzer auf Panther-Fahrgestell (Initial wooden mock-up)

F

Panther Ausf.F (Design proposal/ author's impression)

G

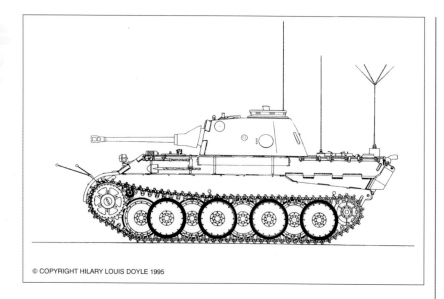

Both the commander and the observer were provided with azimuth indicators to show how far the turret was traversed off the centre of the hull. The commander's indicator was the standard 12-hour ring mounted inside the commander's cupola. The azimuth indicator provided for the observer was located in the front of the turret just below the centre of the range finder. It had two dials. The left-hand dial had an inner scale graduated from 1 to 12 hours and an outer scale graduated in hundreds of mils from 1 to 64. This dial was used for obtaining a rough reading only. A more precise reading could be obtained by using the right-hand dial, which had an outer scale graduated in mils from 0 to 100 and an inner correction disc used for concentrating the fire of a number of different guns on one point.

When a target was sighted, the turret was presumably traversed until the commander was able to lay on the target with the aid of the sighting vane on the cupola. The observers should by then have been able to pick out the target and lay accurately.

An elaborate automatic Blockstelle 0 plotting board made by the firm Anschütz of Kiel was installed in the turret just in front of the commander's cupola. It was primarily an artillery instrument and was intended for use in countries where maps were not available, or were inadequate for artillery use. The Blockstelle was used to give initial range and line to the pivot gun and to give corrections based on observation of the fall of shot. The instrument was used for T.O.B. shoots. The distance OB was measured by the Panzerbeobachtungswagen actually travelling from B to O and the distance OT was determined by using the range finder. The requirement was for equipment able to deal with OB distances up to 12,000 metres in any direction.

The radio sets mounted in the Panzerbeobachtungswagen consisted of an Fu 8, Fu 4, and Funksprechgerät f. The Fu 8 radio set consisted of a 30 watt transmitter with medium wavelength receiver operating in the frequency band of 0.83 to 3 Mhz. The Fu 4 radio set was a medium wavelength receiver operating in the same frequency band, and the Funksprechgerät f radio set could both send and receive in the 19.9 to 21.4 Mhz frequency band.

The Panzerbeobachtungswagen Panther never went into production. As recorded for 31 March 1944 in the war diary of the General der Artillerie OKH, General Lindemann, the issue of Panzers to the artillery had encountered major obstacles. General Thomale (under General Guderian in the Generalinspekteur der Panzertruppen) emphasised that the artillery would not obtain Panthers. The General der Artillerie OKH had briefed the Organizations-Abteilung on the situation, but they were not able to reverse the decision to obtain Panther chassis or components for the artillery.

On 14 May 1944, the Panzerbeobachtungswagen auf Panther-Fahrgestell was included in the list of inventions for the artillery that urgently needed to be pursued.

On 10 November 1944, representatives from Wa Prüf 4 and In 4 (Artillerie) discussed details of a design for an Artillerie-Panzerbeobachtungswagen 'Panther schmal' at Daimler-Benz. The turret was not designed to be traversable. The optical equipment was to consist of seven periscopes in the commander's cupola, a TSR spotting periscope, and a KSFR (box scissors periscope). As conceptually designed, the KSFR was not traversable, so it was only possible to view the area directly to the front, and the commander's cupola hatch could not be closed when the KSFR was installed. The design obviously had to be changed to cut a section out of the hatch cover so that the KSFR could be mounted upright and traversed. Other requested changes included mounting a periscope for the second observer, and connecting both this periscope and the KSFR with a target-indicating device. Radio sets were to be the same as those installed in the Panzerbefehlswagen.

In a meeting with the General der Artillerie OKH on 23 December 1944, General Thomale asked that the request for completion of a Panzerbeobachtungs Panther be temporarily delayed because of the strained production situation. General Thomale was in agreement with producing a Beobachtungswagen auf 38(t) chassis.

PROPOSALS FOR ARTILLERIE SELBSTFAHRLAFETTE

By early 1942, Wa Prüf 4 (the design office for artillery) had already initiated conceptual designs for mounting artillery pieces on self-propelled chassis with automotive components that had been designed for the Panther. Parallel design proposals were prepared by both Fried.Krupp AG, in Essen, and Rheinmetall Borsig, of Düsseldorf

Krupp Proposals

These first Krupp attempts at designing self-propelled artillery pieces which were dismountable from the chassis were identified on 1 July 1942 as the Gerät 5-1528 (s.F.H.43 (Sfl.) Kp.I) Bauelemente Fgst.Panther, and Gerät 5-1211 (12.8 cm K.43 (Sfl.) Kp.I) Bauelemente Fgst.Panther.

The former mounted the 15 cm s.F.H.43 L/35.5, a medium howitzer ordered as a result of experiences gained in Russia. The design was to allow 360 degrees traverse and to have a maximum range of 18,000 metres. An interesting feature was the use of a screw breech, introduced

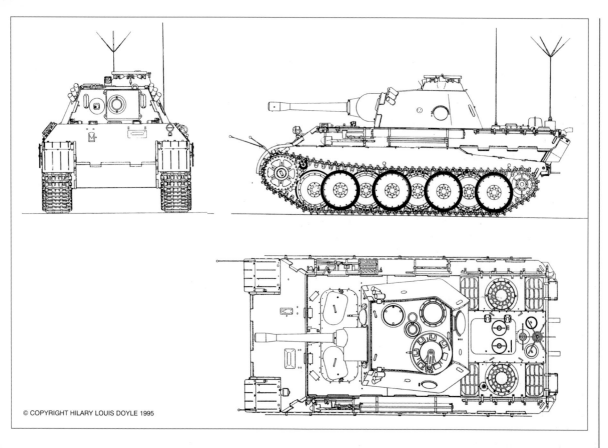

© COPYRIGHT HILARY LOUIS DOYLE 1995

1:76 scale drawing of the Panzerbeobachtungswagen Panther. (Hilary Louis Doyle)

due to the shortage of materials for cartridge case manufacture. The 12.8 cm K.43 proposed by Krupp was also to have 360 degree traverse and the screw breech. Both pieces of equipment had muzzle brakes.

Krupp also embarked on a second series of self-propelled artillery designs identified as the s.F.H.43 Sfl. (Grille 15) and 12.8 cm K.43 Sfl. (Grille 12), and completed a full-scale wooden model in November 1942. The artillery pieces in this proposal were both dismountable and could be traversed through a full circle. The Panther running gear was extended to a wheelbase of 4,200 mm. The wooden models were inspected by Wa Prüf 4 in January 1943. At this time Krupp promised to complete a Versuchs-Grille by 1 September 1943 if the Panther component parts were delivered by 1 May.

On 24 February 1943, Wa Prüf sent Krupp an official list of cover names for their self-propelled artillery:

Cover Name	Applies to
Heuschrecke 12	12.8 cm K43 (Sfl.) Kp.I
Heuschrecke 15	s.F.H.43 (Sfl.) Kp.I
Grille 12	12.8 cm K43 (Sfl.) Kp.II
Grille 15	s.F.H.43 (Sfl.) Kp.II

On 3 April 1943, Wa Prüf 6 informed Krupp that the only Versuchs-Sfl. that was to be completed with Panther components was a single

Grille 12/15. On 5 May 1943, Krupp was notified by Wa Prüf 6 that the contracts for producing two Artillerie-Selbstfahrlafetten Heuschrecke 12 und 15 mit Bauelemente Panther für 12.8 cm K.43 und für s.F.H.43 (dated 8 February 1943) had been cancelled.

On 21 May 1943, M.A.N. was ordered to furnish a single set of the following Panther Ausf.D components needed for the Grille 12/15 to Fried.Krupp AG Essen in July 1943: Gg 24/660/150 tracks, roadwheels, shock absorbers, final drives, track adjusters, Maybach HL 230 engine, AK 7-200 transmission, single-radius steering gear, steering brakes, controls with linkages, brake and transmission fume extraction system, radiators, driver's periscope, and telescoping air intake. (What they wanted with the last component is a complete mystery, because it was only useful in a Panther during submerged fording.)

Krupp reported on 7 June 1943 that a new tenth-scale wooden model of the s.F.H.43 (Sfl.) Grille 15 would be completed by about mid-July. They promised to have the Versuchs-Fahrgestell completed by 1 November 1943. The Panther components were the same for both the 12.8 cm K43 (Sfl.) and the s.F.H.43 (Sfl.) configuration. Sometime after this date the s.F.H.43 and 12.8 cm K.43 were dropped in favour of the more conventional 15 cm s.F.H.44 and the 12.8 cm K.44 L/55 which had a normal breech and electrical firing gear. The latter was basically the same weapon as mounted in the Jagdtiger.

On 20 October 1943, Wa Prüf 4 informed Krupp that in order to further conserve working hours and material, Krupp was to cease all work on the contracts for both design and production of the 12.8 cm

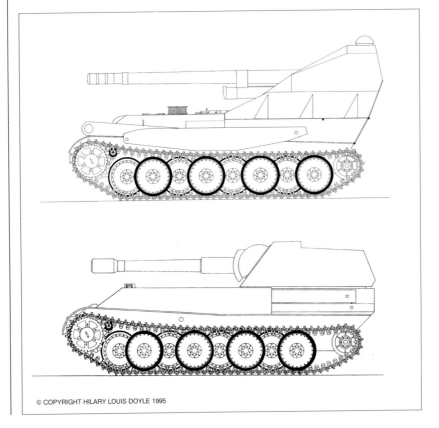

ABOVE, LEFT **1:76 scale side view drawing of the Krupp proposal for 's.F.H.43 (Sfl)' dated 18 January 1943. (Hilary Louis Doyle)**

BELOW, LEFT **1:76 scale side view drawing of the Krupp proposal for 'Sfl mit absetzbarer s.F.H.18' dated 20 January 1944. (Hilary Louis Doyle)**

A model of the Krupp proposal for the 12.8 cm K. 43 (Sfl.) Kp. II, which had the official cover name Grille 12 and was based on Panther components.

K.44 (Sfl.) Grille 12, the s.F.H.44 (Sfl.) Grille 15, the 12.8 cm K.44 (Sfl.) Heuschrecke 12, and the s.F.H.44 (Sfl.) Heuschrecke 15.

Despite these cancellations, Krupp continued to prepare conceptual designs for other self-propelled artillery pieces mounted on chassis utilising Panther components. On 20 January 1944 a new drawing numbered SKA 879 for Sfl. mit absetzbarer s.F.H.18 (dismountable howitzer) shows a 15 cm howitzer, with a muzzle brake, mounted in a compact turret at the rear of the vehicle. A beam either side of the vehicle was attached to this turret. These beams with the turret could be slid rearwards so that the turret could be lowered to the ground. The wheelbase was similar to a normal Panther at 3,920 mm.

A second variant of this conceptual design, Sfl. mit absetzbarer s.F.H.18, was created by Krupp in drawing number SKB 891 dated 3 February 1944. This version featured the turret housing the 15 cm howitzer mounted centrally with the motor compartment at the rear as in a conventional Panther chassis. The apparatus to dismount the turret operated to the front instead of off the rear as had been proposed in the previous design.

Wa Prüf 4 persisted in their attempts to create new designs of self-propelled artillery in mid 1944. On 6 July 1944, a new conceptual design was

The Krupp model proposal for the 12.8 cm K. 43 (Sfl.) Kp. II, the Grille 12, with the firing platform folded down ready for firing.

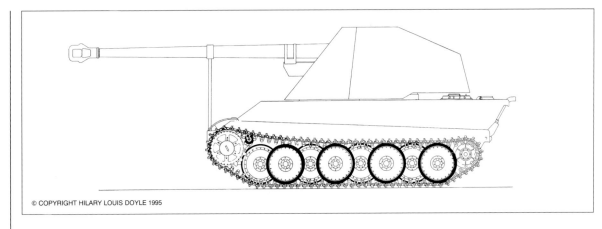

proposed for mounting a 15 cm howitzer on a Panther chassis, traversable through 360 degrees and dismountable, known as the Geschützwagen Panther für s.F.H.18/4 (Sf.).

Krupp's conceptual design, entitled mittlerer Waffenträger, as shown in drawing number Bz 3423 dated 16 September 1944, featured the regular 15 cm s.F.H.18 mounted in a hexagonal turret at the front of a thinly armoured chassis based on Panther components. A second proposal for a mittlerer Waffenträger s.F.H.18/Panther was presented in Krupp drawing number 2.Entwurf No Bz 3423 dated 21 September 1944, and shows a similar turret to the previous design with a regular 15 cm s.F.H.18. However, this turret is mounted in the middle of the vehicle. Krupp also proposed that a 12.8 cm K.44 be mounted on this same chassis and this is shown in drawing number Bz 3428 dated 21 September 1944, entitled 12.8 cm K.44 auf Panther. In order to accommodate this 12.8 cm L/55 gun, which was fitted with a muzzle brake, the turret design was altered by increasing its length and height.

At a meeting with Wa Prüf 4 in Berlin on 22 September 1944, the Krupp representative Dr Bankwitz was informed that there was no longer any interest in the s.F.H.18 auf Pantherfahrzeug and that the Panther was no longer being released for other uses. Apparently undeterred, Krupp created a third proposal by 12 October 1944 shown in drawing number No Bz 3445, entitled mittlerer Waffenträger s.F.H.18/Panther (dünnwandig). This design featured thinner armour and a reduced ammunition load, from 60 to 50 rounds, which resulted in a weight saving of 7 metric tons. The turret was redesigned to be cylindrical in shape.

On 25 October 1944, the General der Artillerie OKH reported that the simplest solution would be to install the 15 cm s.F.H. in a new conceptual design, the schwere Sturmhaubitze (similar to the Jagdpanther). Considerable savings could be realised by eliminating the dismountable requirement. If the howitzer had to be dismounted, however, the battery could tow two wheeled carriages that would enable them to dismount the Panzerhaubitze for lengthy operations. Requirements for traversing through a full circle and dismounting the howitzer resulted in technical difficulties and a complicated weapon. However, the requirement for all-round traverse was absolutely necessary and this proposal was rejected.

On 23 December 1944, General Thomale requested that because of Panther production shortfalls, the General der Artillerie OKH should hold

1:76 scale side view drawing of the Krupp second proposal for 'mittlerer Waffenträger s.F.H.18/Panther' dated 21 September 1944. (Hilary Louis Doyle)

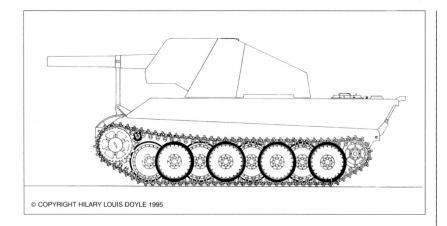

1:76 scale side view drawing of the Krupp proposal for '12.8 cm K44 auf Panther' dated 21 September 1944. (Hilary Louis Doyle)

© COPYRIGHT HILARY LOUIS DOYLE 1995

off on specifications for dismounting and all-round traverse, and wait to see whether a solution would be found for mounting the schwere Panzer-Haubitzen auf Panzer 38 (t) components in the near future. In a telex message dated 6 February 1945 it was reported that the Pantherfahrzeug ohne turm (chassis without turret) required by Habermass of Krupp for the s.Pz.Haubitze was currently at Stahlbau, Hannover.

A report on the development emergency programme dated 20 February 1945 consisted of two lists of inventions that could be progressed. The third list consisted of inventions for which development work was to cease immediately. There was only one invention on the third list from the Panther series: the s.F.H.18 auf Panther-Bauteilen (15 cm howitzer self-propelled chassis designed with Panther components).

Rheinmetall Borsig Proposals

The first Rheinmetall attempts at fulfilling the requirements for a self-propelled artillery piece that could be dismounted from the chassis, was identified on 1 July 1942 as the: Gerät 5-1530 (15 cm s.F.H.43 (Sfl.) Rh.B.) Bauelemente Fgst.Panther, and Gerät 5-1213 (12.8 cm K.43 (Sfl.) Rh.B.) Bauelemente Fgst.Panther

The 12.8 cm K.43 L/51 from Rheinmetall was to be an artillery piece with a carriage allowing 360 degree traverse. It fired a 28 kg round 22,000 metres at a muzzle velocity of 850 m/sec.

Rheinmetall also embarked on a second series of self-propelled artillery designs in which the artillery pieces were mounted in turrets placed in the middle of the vehicle. The turret was dismountable and could be traversed through a full circle both on the vehicle and when dismounted. The chassis has a running gear based on that of the Panther, but extended to a wheelbase of 4,220 mm. These designs were identified as: s.F.H.43 Sfl. drawing number H-SkB 80449 dated 7 January 1943; 12.8 cm K.43 Sfl. drawing number H-SkB 80450 dated 7 January 1943; and 12.8 cm P.43 Sfl. drawing number H-SkB 80451 dated 7 January 1943.

The 15 cm s.F.H.43 L/34 fired a 43.5 kg round 15,000 metres at a muzzle velocity of 600 m/sec. The 12.8 cm P.43 L/54 was a high performance design which fired a sub-calibre round of 14 kg weight at 1,175 m/sec. Rheinmetall promised to complete their first Versuchs-Grille by 1 August 1943 if they received the Panther components by 1 April.

Further design work by Rheinmetall produced the following proposals: 12.8 cm Skorpian (Panther Bauteilen) drawing number H-SKA

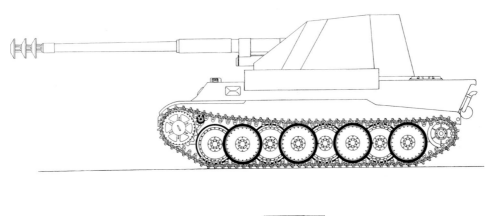

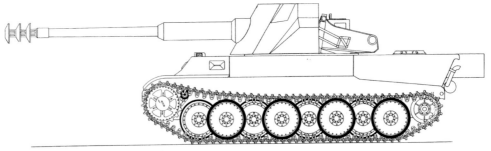

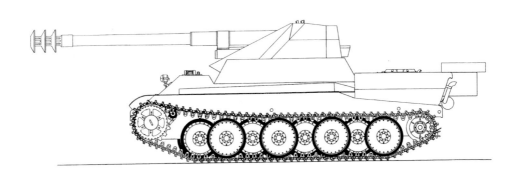

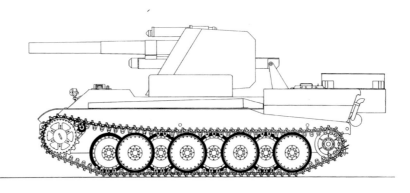

81959 dated 2 April 1943, and s.F.H.43 Sfl. mit Panther-Bauteilen drawing number H-SKA 82566 dated 16 April 1943. These designs feature a chassis with a wheelbase of 4,025 mm which was used, with minor variation, for all subsequent Rheinmetall proposals.

After Wa Prüf 4 cancelled the initial Grille, Heuschrecke and Skorpian series of conceptual designs in the autumn of 1943, Rheinmetall proposed a new series of self-propelled artillery pieces on chassis utilising Panther components in 1944.

In drawing number H-SKA 86187 dated 11 January 1944, Rheinmetall presented a conceptual design for an s.F.H.18 mounted on a chassis utilising Panther components. The third proposal for this conceptual design was shown in drawing number H-SKA 88200 dated 31 January 1944 and entitled s.F.H.18 Sfl. auf Panther Bauteilen. In this revised proposal the firing height of the 15 cm s.F.H.18 at zero degrees elevation had been increased from 2,500 metres to 2.750 metres in an attempt to allow increased elevation.

There are no records that show whether Rheinmetall responded to the Wa Prüf 4 conceptual design of 6 July 1944 known as Geschützwagen Panther für s.F.H.18/4 (Sf.), or if they were involved on subsequent attempts to mount artillery weapons on Panthers.

In a drawing dated September 1943 Rheinmetall proposed that two Panther chassis be used to carry a super heavy artillery piece, the 28 cm L/52 gun, which would be suspended between the two vehicles during transport. It was envisaged that the gun platform be lowered to the ground for firing, and the Panther chassis driven away. The title of the drawings was 28 cm DueKa auf Panther Langholzprinzip, but nothing came of this proposal.

PROPOSALS FOR FLAKPANZER

In 1941, Krupp began designing a Versuchsflakwagen (VFW) as a self-propelled mount for the 8.8 cm Flak L/71 anti-aircraft gun. The initial design had all new automotive components which had not been tested previously in other armoured vehicles. In another attempt at design unification, Wa Prüf 6 directed that the chassis for all newly-designed, fully-tracked armoured vehicles should be restricted to component parts from the Luchs, Leopard, Panther, or Tiger. On 2 September 1942, Krupp discussed the redesign of the Versuchsflakwagen (VFW) Gerät 42, which was based on Leopard components with one exception: the suspension was to have the smaller diameter roadwheels and wider track from the Panther.

By 4 November 1942, the entire automotive design for the series production version of the Gerät 42 was based on components from the M.A.N. Panther. The parts needed included the suspension, track adjusters, final drives, steering gears, hand and foot controls and linkages, AK 7-200 transmission, and the Maybach HL 230 engine. The redesigned self-propelled chassis known as the Gerät 42 (VFW II) had the exact same superstructure as the original VFW with hinged sides. No alterations were to be allowed until experience was gained from testing the original VFW. Further changes in the chassis design were discussed, and on 22 October 1943 Krupp reported that the basis for the VFW II

OPPOSITE **1:76 scale side view drawing of the Rheinmetall proposal for '12.8 cm K43 (Sfl)' dated 7 January 1943. (Hilary Louis Doyle)**

1:76 scale side view drawing of the Rheinmetall proposal for '12.8 cm Scorpion (Panther Bauteilen)' dated 2 April 1943. (Hilary Louis Doyle)

1:76 scale side view drawing of the Rheinmetall proposal for '15 cm s.F.H.43 mit Panther-Bauteilen' dated 16 April 1943. (Hilary Louis Doyle)

1:76 scale side view drawing of the Rheinmetall proposal for 's.F.H.18 auf Panther Bauteilen' dated 31 January 1944. (Hilary Louis Doyle)

should now be the Panther II. Components for the Panther II were to be delivered and the Panther I chassis that had already arrived for conversion could be sent back. Decisions on the new design were to await the demonstration of the VFW in November.

Rheinmetall Borsig, meanwhile, had been progressing with their 8.8 cm Flak 41 (Sf) mit Panther I Bauteile (8.8 cm Flak 41, Self-propelled, with Panther I components). A series of drawings dated 12-24 October 1943 clearly showed the main features of the design.

The chassis had Panther components, including the suspension, track adjusters, final drives, steering gears, hand and foot controls and linkages, AK 7-200 transmission, and the Maybach HL 230 engine. The wheelbase was increased to 4,025 mm and the overall vehicle was considerably longer than a normal Panther. From early 1943 this chassis had been under design as a self-propelled mount to carry a variety of artillery pieces. In the October drawings, the 8.8 cm Flak 41 L/74 was to be mounted in a large turret from which it could be removed and placed on the ground. Four outriggers were provided which could be attached to the pedestal base to provide stability.

1:76 scale side view drawing of the Rheinmetall-Borsig proposal for '8.8 cm Flak 41 (Sf) mit Panther I Bauteilen' dated 24 October 1943. (Hilary Louis Doyle)

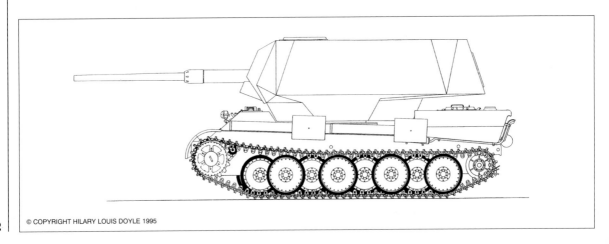

A model of an 8.8 cm Flakwagen based on Panther components. This design project by Rheinmetall-Borsig, started in November 1942, was cancelled in January 1944.

The only information on the progress on the Rheinmetall design came from Krupp, who reported on 13 January 1944 that Rheinmetall had very significant problems to overcome in the design of a turret for an 8.8 cm Flak 41 auf Sfl.

On the same day, at a separate meeting, Krupp and Rheinmetall were ordered to cease development of the 8.8 cm Flak 41 auf Selbstfahrlafette f.r Panzer IV und Panther I because more urgent designs needed the limited manpower. It was decided that the 8.8 cm Flakwagen for escorting Panzers was unnecessary because high-flying aircraft could also be engaged by stationary 8.8 cm Flak guns located off to the side. Instead, defence against ground-strafing aircraft was needed, particularly from 3.7 cm or 5.5 cm Flak, and armour protection on the top of the Flakpanzers was also necessary.

The methods and tactics for anti-aircraft defence for Panzers had already been discussed in detail on 31 May 1943, and the conclusion was that Flakpanzers were needed. At first, the German army would attempt to adopt the Pz.Kpfw.IV chassis as a Flakpanzer. If this failed, they would fall back on the Panther chassis. The 2 cm Flakvierling (quad mount) and the single-barrel 3.7 cm Flak were proposed for mounting on the Pz.Kpfw.IV chassis. A 2 cm Flakvierling (quad without carriage), a 3.7 cm Flakzwilling (twin) or 3.7 cm Flakdrilling (triple), and, after completion of its development, a 5.5 cm Flakzwilling were proposed as the armament to be mounted on the Panther chassis.

On 24 May 1943 Rheinmetall's drawing H-SKA 82827 introduced their proposal for Turm Panther II mit Vierling MG151/20. This was a heavily armoured turret with two pairs of the MG151/20 offset and at different heights. This configuration never reached any advanced stage.

When the Panzerkommission met on 21 December 1943, they decided that the 3.7 cm Flak auf Panzer IV and the 3 cm Doppelflak U-Boot Turm auf Panzer IV were transitional solutions. The final solution was a new design for a 3.7 cm Doppelflak auf Panther, in which provision was to be made for later switching to a 5.5 cm Flak. Daimler-Benz was selected to design a 3.7 cm Flak-Zwilling turret that could be mounted on the Panther chassis.

The model of an 8.8 cm Flakwagen based on Panther components with the gun elevated.

43

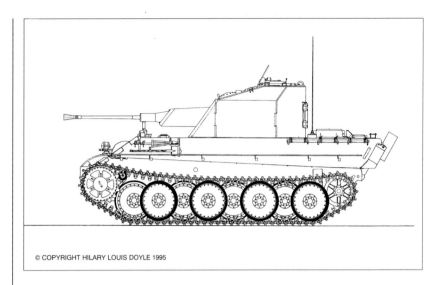

1:76 scale side view drawing of the Rheinmetall proposal for 'Flakpanzer 341' dated May 1944. (Hilary Louis Doyle)

Armour protection was 100 mm thick on the front of the turret, and 40 mm thick on the sides. The hydraulic drive for traversing the turret was to be powered off the Panther's engine. Considerable design problems had be solved, including expelling spent propellant fumes, controlling back-flaming from the gun breech, and sighting and acquiring targets from within a closed turret. Daimler-Benz was to complete a Versuchs-Turm by the middle of the year.

During 1944, design work on a 3.7 cm Flakzwilling turret was also assigned to Vereinigte Apparatebau AG, a subsidiary of Rheinmetall-Borsig. In a series of detailed drawings dated May 1944, they outlined their proposals for Flakpanzer 341. The designation referred to the twin 3.7 cm Flak 341, which were high performance versions of the 3.7 cm Flak 43 ordered by the Marineamt in 1941.

On 13 January 1945, Wa Prüf 6 informed the designers that the Generalinspekteur der Panzertruppen had decided to cancel installation of the 3.7 cm Flakzwilling 44 in a turret on the Panther chassis because the fire power in relation to the weight of the vehicle was far too low. Therefore, design work was stopped despite the project's advanced stage.

The firm of Vereinigte Apparatebau were also selected to design a turret for the Flakpanzer V, 5.5 cm Zwilling, Gerät 58. They presented their conceptual design drawings and a tenth-scale model to Wa Prüf 6 on 8 November 1944. After a discussion of detail changes, Vereinigte Apparatebau received a contract to quickly complete a full-scale wooden model of a 5.5 cm Flakpanzerturm. In order to ensure that weapons were available in time for installation in an armoured turret, Wa Pr f 6 gave a contract to the firm of Dürkoppwerke for two right-hand and two left-hand guns.

Vereinigte Apparatebau met on 19 December 1944 to discuss further design development on the 5.5 cm Flakpanzer. They were to try to mount the following weapons in the gun mantlet on top of the twin 5.5 cm guns: either two MG151/20 and one MG42, or two MG42 and one MG151/20, or two MG151/20 without an MG42. They were also to contact Wa Prüf 6 to find an existing motor to drive the hydraulic traverse. The commander's cupola was to be similar to the commander's cupola on the Panther. Two wooden tenth-scale models of the

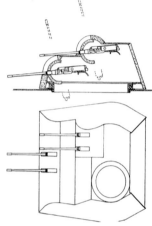

1:76 scale drawing of the Rheinmetall proposal for 'Turm Panther II mit Vierling MG151/20' dated 20 May 1943. (Hilary Louis Doyle)

A wooden mock-up of the 3.7 cm Flakpanzer 341 turret on a Panther chassis. (Bundesarchiv)

1:76 scale side view drawing of the Rheinmetall proposal for '5.5 cm Flakpanzer' dated November 1944. (Hilary Louis Doyle)

Flakpanzer were to be delivered to Wa Prüf 6. Krupp also put forward their proposal for a 5.5 cm Zwilling Flakpanzer in drawing No Bz 3476 dated 5 December 1944.

On 14 February 1945, Oberst. Crohn of Wa Prüf 6 decided that the development work on the 5.5 cm Flakpanzer had no place in the emergency programme and was to be halted. Work on the wooden model by the Vereinigte Apparatebau was to be completed and Wa Prüf 6 informed when the model could be displayed.

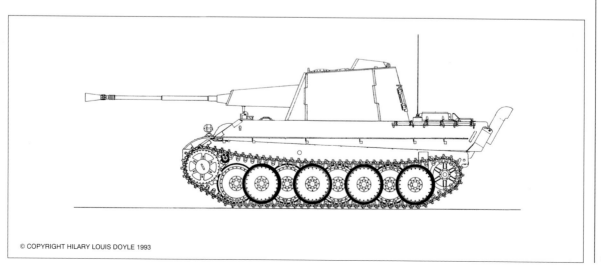

THE PLATES

A1: PANTHER AUSF.A AS A PANZER-BEFEHLSWAGEN, PANZER-REGIMENT 4, ANZIO, ITALY, 1944

This Panzerbefehlswagen was assembled by M.A.N. in October/November 1943 and was one of the 76 Panthers brought to Italy by the I.Abteilung/Panzer-Regiment 4 in February 1944. This unit was part of a task force of heavy armour assigned to tackle the Allied bridgehead at Anzio. This Panther Ausf.A still had the TZF12 binocular gunsight, pistol ports on the turret sides, and the 'letterbox' machine gun port in the glacis plate. As a Panzerbefehlswagen, it had no coaxial machine gun, and the opening in the gun mantlet was plugged. This was an Sd.Kfz.267 which was equipped with the Fu 8 radio set in the hull and the Fu 5 in the turret. An armour cylinder was welded onto the rear deck to protect the porcelain insulator mount for the Sternantenne d for the Fu 8 radio set. The mount for the 2 m rod antenna for the Fu 5 radio set was located on the right rear corner of the turret roof.

From September 1943 to September 1944 all Panthers had a coating of Zimmerit (anti-magnetic paste) applied at the assembly plant. A base coat of dunkelgelb RAL 7028 (tan) paint was sprayed over the undercoat and Zimmerit at the assembly plants. The units were authorised to apply camouflage patterns of stripes and patches of olivgrün RAL 6003 (dark olive green) and rotbraun RAL 8017 (dark chocolate brown) over the base coat of dunkelgelb RAL 7028. The tactical number 102, in red outlined in white, was repeated in numbers 35 cm high on either side and on the rear of the turret.

A2: PANTHER AUSF.G MIT FG 1250, OCTOBER 1944

This Panther Ausf.G was built in October 1944 with all the modifications necessary for mounting night fighting equipment: infra-red sights and illumination devices. The FG 1250, consisting of an infra-red sight and searchlight, was mounted in the commander's cupola and slaved to the main gun. A GG 400 auxiliary generator was carried inside the fighting compartment replacing the right rear ammunition stowage bin (three rounds).

Camouflage was applied at the factory: a thin coat of base red primer rot RAL 8012 was over-painted with well thinned stripes and patches, with sharp outlines, of dunkelgelb RAL 7028 (tan) and olivgrün RAL 6003 (dark olive green). To simulate sunlight passing through foliage, all dark areas were painted with spots of dunkelgelb RAL 7028. Spots of olivgrün RAL 6003 and rot RAL 8012 were applied to the dunkelgelb RAL 7028 areas, green nearest the green areas and red-brown near the red primer base.

B1: BERGEPANTHER, SEPTEMBER 1943

This Bergepanther, based on the Panther Ausf.D (Fgst.Nr. 212161), was built by Henschel in September 1943. It was used as a test vehicle.

The exterior was painted in the dunkelgelb RAL 7028 (tan applied from February 1943). The units were authorised to apply camouflage patterns of stripes and patches of olivgrün RAL 6003 (dark olive green) and rotbraun RAL 8017 (dark chocolate brown) over the base coat of dunkelgelb RAL 7028.

B2: PANTHER OSTWALLTURM, GOTHIC LINE, ITALY 1944

The Pantherturm I (Stahluntersatz) was mounted on a welded steel base in which the ammunition was stored. This base was in turn bolted on to the top of a steel box which housed the crew living quarters, stove and electric generator equipment. Although some normal Pz.Kpfw.Panther turrets had been used for these fixed fortifications on the Hitler Line south of Cassino, the majority, such as this one on the Gothic Line, were specially designed and produced for this purpose. The roof armour was increased to 40 mm to withstand direct hits from 150 mm artillery shells, and the cupola was replaced by a flat hatch with a rotating periscope.

The Panther Ostwallturm was painted at the factory with a coat of base red primer rot RAL 8012. On deployment the turret was painted with stripes and patches of dunkelgelb RAL 7028 (tan) and olivgrün RAL 6003 (dark olive green). The interior was painted in elfenbein RAL 1001 (ivory).

C: JAGDPANTHER, ARDENNES, DECEMBER 1944

This Jagdpanther (Fgst.Nr. 303018) was completed at MNH, Hannover, at the end of November or the beginning of December 1944 and issued to a schwere Heeres-Panzerjäger-Abteilung which took part in the Ardennes Offensive. It was captured by the US Forces and shipped to Aberdeen Proving Ground where it is still on display. This particular Jagdpanther still had the small diameter idlerwheel. It was also one of a small series which had the fighting compartment exhaust fan mounted over the main gun.

The camouflage pattern was applied at the factory and only partially covered the base coat of primer rot RAL 8012 (red). Well thinned dunkelgelb RAL 7028 (tan) was painted in vertical stripes, flanked by stripes of thinned weiss RAL 9002 (white).

D: PANTHER AUSF.G MIT FG 1250, OCTOBER 1944

Built in October 1944, this Panther Ausf.G was modified for night fighting with infra-red sights and illumination devices. The FG 1250, consisting of an infra-red sight and searchlight, was mounted in the commander's cupola and slaved to the main gun. The right rear ammunition stowage bin inside the fighting compartment was replaced by a GG 400 auxiliary generator.

The camouflage was applied at the factory and consists of a thin coat of base red primer rot RAL 8012 with over-painted with well thinned stripes and patches, with sharp outlines, of dunkelgelb RAL 7028 (tan) and olivgrün RAL 6003 (dark olive green). All dark areas were painted with spots of dunkelgelb RAL 7028 to simulate sunlight passing through foliage. Spots of olivgrün RAL 6003 and rot RAL 8012 were applied to the dunkelgelb RAL 7028 areas, green nearest the green areas and red-brown near the red primer base.

The interior of the fighting compartment was painted in elfenbein RAL 1001 (ivory). Radio sets were dunkelgrau RAL 7021 (dark grey). The motor compartment was left in primer rot RAL 8012 (dried blood red). The 7.5 cm Panzergranate 39 (A.P.C.B.C./H.E. shell) was identified by having the projectile painted schwarz RAL 9005 (black) with a weiss RAL 9002 (white) cap. The 7.5 cm Sprenggranate (high explosive shell) was painted in olivgrün RAL 6003 (dark olive green). Most of the 7.5 cm Kw.K.42 ammunition was manufactured from steel rather than brass shell cases due to shortages of materials.

E: PANZERBEOBACHTUNGSWAGEN PANTHER, 1943

The Artillerie requested an armoured observation vehicle with the characteristics of a battle tank which could replace the lightly armoured Beobachtungswagen based on the semi-track chassis. Initially, a series of Panzerbeobachtungswagen were created using rebuilt Pz.Kpfw.III. But the Artillerie wanted a larger vehicle based on the new Panther chassis. Design work was completed and a Versuchssturm (experimental turret) was mounted on a Panther chassis to undergo tests. Due to the high demand for Panthers for the Panzertruppe, the Artillerie were not allowed to order series production for the Panzerbeobachtungswagen Panther.

The chassis of this Versuchs-Panzerbeobachtungswagen Panther was produced in July-August 1943. Tanks of this period were painted in a base coat of dunkelgelb RAL 7028 (tan). As an experimental vehicle there was no need to issue the olivgrün RAL 6003 (dark olive green) and rotbraun RAL 8017 (dark chocolate brown) paste used by the field units to apply camouflage patterns.

F: 3.7 CM FLAKPANZER AUF PANTHER-FAHRGESTELL

On 21 December 1943, the Panzerkommission chose the 3.7 cm Doppelflak auf Panther to provide anti-aircraft defence of Panzer formations. Initially, Daimler-Benz was entrusted with the design of the turret, but during 1944 the work was reassigned to Vereinigte Apparatebau A.G. Detailed design progressed and a wooden mock-up was prepared. However, on 13 January 1945 it was decided the fire power was too

low in relation to the weight of the vehicle, and work on the installation of the 3.7 cm Flakzwilling 44 in a turret on the Panther chassis was suspended. Efforts were to be concentrated instead on a 5.5 cm Flakzwilling turret.

To aid in detailed design work, a full-scale wooden mock-up of the turret was mounted on a Panther chassis. The finished production turret was to have had many changes incorporated, including sloped frontal armour. This full-scale wooden mock on the Panther chassis was painted in dunkelgelb RAL 7028 (tan).

G: PANTHER AUSF.F

The Panther Ausf.F was designed as a new turret, the Schmalturm, on a slightly modified Panther Ausf.G chassis. Photographs show Panther Ausf.F chassis and turrets already in production in Daimler-Benz in April 1945, but there is no evidence that final assembly of any series production Panther Ausf.F was completed. If the turrets had been mounted on completed chassis, they would have lacked the optical components. Our colour plate shows how a Panther Ausf.F might have looked had any been completed.

At the beginning of February 1945, orders were issued for the assembly plants to apply a base coat of olivgrün RAL 6003 (dark olive green) to new production equipment. An original colour photograph of a Tiger Ausf.B, completed in March 1945, reveals that dunkelgelb RAL 7028 (tan) was applied in stripes and patches to create a camouflage pattern over the base coat of olivgrün RAL 6003 (dark olive green).

BELOW **The Panther and Jagdpanther assembly lines at MNH in Hannover after it was captured in 1945. (Tank Museum)**

INDEX

(References to illustrations are shown in **bold**. Plates are shown with caption locators in brackets.)